W9-AHC-248

SPENCER LOOMIS SCHOOL
1 Hubbard Lane
Hawthorn Woods, IL 60047

Biomes
of the World

CHAPARRAL

EDWARD R. RICCIUTI

BENCHMARK BOOKS

MARSHALL CAVENDISH
NEW YORK

Benchmark Books
Marshall Cavendish Corporation
99 White Plains Road
Tarrytown, New York 10591-9001

©Marshall Cavendish Corporation, 1996

Series created by Blackbirch Graphics, Inc.

Printed in Hong Kong.

Library of Congress Cataloging-in-Publication Data

Ricciuti, Edward R.
    Chaparral / by Edward R. Ricciuti.
        p.   cm. — (Biomes of the world)
    Includes bibliographical references (p.   ) and index.
    Summary: Defines chaparral biomes and covers where they are located as well as the plants and animals that inhabit them.
        ISBN 0-7614-0137-7 (lib. bdg.)
    1. Chaparral ecology—Juvenile literature. 2. Chaparral—Juvenile literature. [1. Chaparral. 2. Chaparral ecology. 3. Ecology.] I. Title. II. Series.
QH541.5.c5R535   1996
574.5'2652—dc20   95-41071
                                                                                    CIP
                                                                                    AC

Contents

Introduction   4

1. The In-Between Biome   7

2. Plants of the Chaparral   17

3. Fire and the Chaparral   27

4. Wildlife of the Chaparral   37

5. The Chaparral and People   51

   Glossary   60

   For Further Reading   61

   Index   62

Introduction

People traveling in an airplane often marvel at the patchwork patterns they see as they look down on the land. Fields, forests, grasslands, and deserts, each with its own identifiable color and texture, form a crazy quilt of varying designs. Ecologists—scientists who study the relationship between living things and their environment—have also observed the repeating patterns of life that appear across the surface of the earth. They have named these geographical areas biomes. A biome is defined by certain environmental conditions and by the plants and animals that have adapted to these conditions.

The map identifies the earth's biomes and shows their placement across the continents. Most of the biomes are on land. They include the tropical rainforest, temperate forest, grassland, tundra, taiga, chaparral, and desert. Each has a unique climate, including yearly patterns of temperature, rainfall, and sunlight, as well as certain kinds of soil. In addition to the land biomes, the oceans of the world make up a single biome, which is defined by its salt-water environment.

Looking at biomes helps us understand the interconnections between our planet and the living things that inhabit it. For example, the tilt of the earth on its axis and wind patterns both help to determine the climate of any particular biome.

The climate, in turn, has a great impact on the types of plants that can flourish, or even survive, in an area. That plant life influences the composition and stability of the soil. And the soil, in turn, influences which plants will thrive. These interconnections continue in every aspect of nature. While some animals eat plants, others use plants for shelter or concealment. And the types of plants that grow in a biome directly influence the species of animals that live there. Some of the animals help pollinate plants. Many of them enrich the soil with their waste.

Within each biome, the interplay of climatic conditions, plants, and animals defines a broad pattern of life. All of these interactions make the plants and animals of a biome interdependent and create a delicate natural balance. Recognizing these different relationships and how they shape the natural world enables us to appreciate the complexity of life on Earth and the beauty of the biomes of which we are a part.

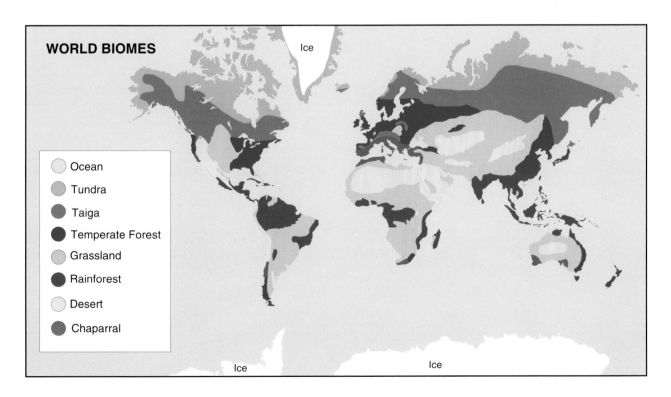

WORLD BIOMES

Ice

- Ocean
- Tundra
- Taiga
- Temperate Forest
- Grassland
- Rainforest
- Desert
- Chaparral

Ice   Ice

1

The In-Between Biome

Chaparral is the name for dense thickets of low trees and shrubs that are adapted to surviving fire, heat, and drought. Found in only a few places in the world and not nearly as extensive as the other biomes, such as the grassland and the desert, it is the world's smallest biome. Even where chaparral grows, in fact, it often does so in patches surrounded by other types of vegetation.

For many reasons, the chaparral could be called the "in-between biome." It often grows between desert and grassland, or forest and grassland, and shares certain characteristics with those biomes. Chaparral is found only in specific areas,

Opposite: The shrubby plants of the chaparral grow in many different types of terrain. Here, the chaparral thrives on the Mediterranean island of Corsica.

7

Scrub oak is a common plant of the California and Mediterranean chaparral.

between regions with a hot, dry climate and high atmospheric pressure, and regions with a cool, wet climate and low atmospheric pressure. Those places where chaparral thrives have hot, dry summers and mild, wet winters. Scientists describe this type of climate as Mediterranean.

The chaparral biome is the one that has been the least studied by scientists, and thus it can seem a place of mystery. Some parts of the chaparral look almost like a wasteland, while other areas resemble immense wild gardens that are ablaze with brilliant flowers. This biome is subject to great extremes of climate and is shaped by a force that both destroys and renews it—fire.

What Is Chaparral?

There are many types of chaparral. The most common is the dwarf evergreen forest. Few of the trees exceed 10 feet (3 meters) in height, and most are smaller than that. They are closely packed together and in some cases form stands that are so thick that people and large animals have difficulty penetrating them. The species of trees found in the chaparral differ geographically. In the Mediterranean and California chaparral, for example, many of the trees are scrub oaks; in Australia, they are dwarf eucalyptus.

The chaparral also contains flowers and many thickets of shrubs, which are often thorny. In some places, the shrubs almost completely cover the landscape, replacing the trees. In other places, the shrubs are widely spaced and are separated by patches of various types of grasses, which cannot survive where shrubs and trees are tightly massed.

Most plants of the chaparral have tough, leathery leaves. Many have thorns and are gnarled and twisted. They grow in many different types of terrain: flat plains, as in Australia; jagged, rocky hills cut by canyons, as on such Mediterranean islands as Corsica; and the lower slopes of snowy mountain peaks, as in the Sierra Nevada of California.

Opposite:
A manzanita
tree blooms on
Kitt's Peak in
Arizona.

Where Is the Chaparral?

Scientists generally agree that the chaparral exists in five different areas of the world: western North America, from southwestern Oregon through California to Baja California; central Chile; the coasts around much of the Mediterranean Sea; southwestern Australia; and the Cape of Good Hope at the southern tip of South Africa.

If you have seen Western movies or television series, particularly reruns from the 1940s and 1950s, it is likely that you have seen the chaparral. Many of them were filmed in the California chaparral, which is close to Hollywood yet looks like the "Wild West."

There is also vegetation in the mountains of central Arizona, between 4,000 and 6,000 feet (1,220 and 1,830 meters) in elevation, that many scientists consider to be chaparral. It lies between the hot dry deserts of the lowlands and the cold, moist forests of the slopes above. Although some scientists consider these parts of Arizona to be within the chaparral biome, others do not. They argue that the Arizona vegetation differs from chaparral in that it is well inland. More often than not, chaparral grows in regions that border an ocean, such as California and the southern tip of Africa.

In many areas, chaparral is scattered among other types of vegetation. On the southern coast of Spain, in and near the delta of the Guadalquivir River, lies one of the last true wildernesses of southern Europe. Part of this area, Parque Nacional de Doñana, shelters wildlife that has vanished from most of the rest of the continent. Parque Nacional de Doñana contains marshes and vast pinewoods, but the largest expanse of vegetation there is the heath, which is made up of thickets of plants called halimium that grow about 5 feet (1.5 meters) high. Scattered throughout the heath is macchia, as one sort of chaparral is called in Europe. In California, chaparral is often found among forests of pine or large oaks, as well as near grasslands and scrub-covered deserts.

Betwixt and Between

Two belts of very high atmospheric pressure ring the globe. One is in the Northern Hemisphere, and the other is in the Southern Hemisphere. Each belt is on a latitude of between 30° and 35° and produces a hot, dry climate. For example, the northern belt has created the Sahara Desert, in northern Africa, and the southern belt has formed the blistering Kalahari Desert, which is also in Africa.

Mediterranean chaparral lies between the northern belt and the cool, moist climate of central Europe. The chaparral of South Africa lies between the southern belt and the cold South Atlantic Ocean. Other areas of chaparral grow either north of the northern belt or south of the southern belt.

Chaparral Climate

During the course of a year, the climate in most areas of the chaparral varies greatly. Indeed, the weather can change sharply in a matter of days. Temperatures in the California chaparral, for instance, average from 50°F to 60°F (10°C to 15°C) during the winter but can quickly drop to near freezing. Occasionally, hard frosts occur. Summer temperatures can send the mercury soaring to 100°F (38°C) and higher. When temperatures rise, the chaparral becomes desert-dry, with only a trace of moisture in the air.

Most of the rain that falls on the chaparral comes from storms that begin over the Pacific Ocean, including those that start with areas of low atmospheric pressure in the far north. Almost all of that rainfall occurs between late fall and early spring. A few raindrops may fall in November. December often brings a few days of rain, and January even more. By February, the rains are at their peak, and the chaparral gets a dousing. Precipitation then begins to dwindle until it disappears, by May. During the summer, an area of permanent high atmospheric pressure prevents ocean storms from moving over the chaparral.

Many plants of the chaparral are the same species as those found in nearby deserts. Others, which are not found in deserts, have adaptations for surviving during droughts similar to those adaptations that have evolved among many desert species.

One main adaptation that is prevalent among chaparral flora is dwarfing. There are a number of reasons for this adaptation—severe drought and extreme changes of climate being just two of them. Another reason for dwarfing is the chaparral's poor soil. Even when it rains, the soil is not very fertile and it is only able to hold moisture for a short time. In addition, because the chaparral is so dry, great wildfires periodically sweep through it. These wildfires help keep the trees of the chaparral stunted. They also clear away old growth and allow new plants to flourish.

Chaparral Wildlife

Since the chaparral is so widely scattered around the world, it is a biome that contains many different types and groups of animals. These animals range from elephants in South Africa to condors in California to kangaroos in Australia. Moreover, because the chaparral shares so many characteristics with the desert, forest, and, to a certain extent, grassland biomes, most animals that live within it also inhabit one or more of these other environments.

Wildlife has dwindled in many parts of the chaparral because some of these areas, such as the Mediterranean coast of Europe and coastal California, have become heavily populated by people. The balance of nature is fragile in the chaparral, as in the other biomes, and it is greatly affected by many human activities. In the Mediterranean region in particular, chaparral has replaced great forests of tall oaks. These huge stands of oak forests were destroyed centuries ago by human activities that included such things as clearing land for both lumbering and grazing purposes.

Elephants wander through the South African chaparral.

Chaps and Bandits

The chaparral biome is called by different names in different parts of the world. The name chaparral comes from a word used by the Basque people, who were originally from the Pyrenees Mountains between France and Spain. They used the word chabarra to describe dwarf evergreen oaks. The Spanish used a similar word, chaparro, for the same vegetation. When the Spanish came to the New World, chaparro became chaparral, which means a place where small evergreen oaks are located.

A cowboy sports leather chaps, named for the chaparral, in an illustration by Frederic Remington.

Chaps, the word for the leather leggings traditionally worn by cowboys to protect their legs from thorny, thick vegetation, comes from the word chaparral.

In Australia, chaparral is called mallee scrub, after a type of small eucalyptus tree that is common there. South African chaparral is called fynbos. Chaparral in Europe is known as garigue and macchia, or maquis. The last name was once given to bandits who would hide from the authorities in the dense chaparral. French underground resistance fighters who opposed the Nazis during World War II were also called maquis.

2

Plants of the Chaparral

Not all chaparral flora is the same. The communities of plants in the chaparral differ in distant regions as well as locally, according to the particular type of environment in which they grow. All chaparral plants, however, must cope with the difficult climatic conditions described in the preceding chapter.

The Many Faces of Chaparral

Scientists have divided chaparral into many different types. The look of the vegetation and the species that comprise it are two criteria they use to classify chaparral. Not all scientists agree on how many types there are, or what to call them. The scientists, however, do agree on many of them.

The most common type of chaparral is that with a dense cover of large shrubs and scattered scrub and cork oaks, some reaching 10 feet (3 meters) high. This sort of chaparral is usually called maquis in Europe. It is known as chamiso-redshank chaparral in California, after the most widespread shrubs found there. Chamiso is so abundant, in fact, that in some areas it is almost the only shrub to be found.

Chamiso-redshank chaparral, however, does contain other shrubs, such as poison oak, sugar sumac, and manzanita, as well as small scrub oaks. Scrub oaks produce a huge amount of acorns. Thus, they have a greater chance of reproducing in the extreme climate and poor soil of the chaparral. An acre of scrub oaks may yield as much as 10 tons (9 metric tons) of acorns in a single year.

One of the main plants in the maquis, or European chaparral, is the Scotch broom. The maquis also contains many small oaks, wild olive trees, and wiry shrubs, such as white shadbush and yellow gorse. Yellow gorse has been introduced into California, where it has spread rapidly through the native chaparral.

Scotch broom, with its striking yellow flowers, is a common plant both in the European and California chaparral.

PLANTS THAT FEED ON OTHER PLANTS

Several plants of the chaparral are parasites. Most parasitic plants lack chlorophyll. To nourish themselves, they take their nutrients and water from other plants, to which they attach themselves. A parasite common in the California chaparral is a vine called the dodder. More than twenty species of dodder inhabit the California chaparral.

The dodder begins life as the rainy season winds down. It sprouts from a seed that has dropped to the ground. The young vine, which is rooted in the ground, starts to climb. It attaches itself to a larger plant with suckers and begins feeding. As the dodder obtains food from its host plant, its base withers and detaches from the ground. The plant on which the dodder feeds eventually dies. However, in the close-packed world of the chaparral, the dodder can easily reach out and attach itself to another host.

Another parasitic plant is the mistletoe, which is commonly used as a Christmas decoration. It is found in the chaparral as well as in other biomes. The mistletoe has chlorophyll, so it can make its own food, but it gets water from its host. It can drink so much water that its host dies. Mistletoes are often found on oaks, which is why the chaparral is a good home for them.

Masses of the parasite plant mistletoe crowd a live oak tree.

Another type of chaparral found in Europe, garigue, grows in soils that are thin, stony, and poor in nutrients. Garigue often occurs where human activities have destroyed maquis. It contains scattered, low shrubs with stiff, woody branches, as well as herbs, such as rosemary and thyme.

Some scientists consider a California plant community known as coastal scrub to be a form of chaparral. It grows along a narrow strip along the ocean and reaches a maximum height of about 7 feet (2 meters). Like garigue in Europe, coastal scrub often invades areas where people have disturbed

The bitter cherry shrub, with its bright red fruit, grows in the montane chaparral.

the environment. Coastal scrub is a mix of many different plant species, including sagebrush, coyote brush, poison oak, and chaparral yucca.

Two types of chaparral that grow on mountain slopes in California are among the thickest found anywhere. They can be so dense that large creatures, such as deer, cannot travel through them. Mixed chaparral, which generally does not grow more than 15 feet (5 meters) high, covers steep slopes up to an elevation of 5,500 feet (1,678 meters). Among its most common trees are scrub oaks and chaparral oaks, as well as a few dwarf coniferous pines. Its shrubs include manzanita, chamiso, and mountain mahogany. Montane, or mountain, chaparral covers slopes from 3,000 to 9,000 feet (915 to 2,745 meters), and is sometimes mixed with coniferous trees. Montane chaparral grows about 10 feet (3 meters) high and consists mostly of large shrubs, such as manzanita, whitethorn ceanothus, and bitter cherry.

The mallee scrub of Australia and the fynbos of South Africa are examples of a more open type of chaparral. On mallee plains, scattered dwarf eucalyptus trees, many no more than 10 feet (3 meters) tall, grow above a low cover of shrubs and grasses, such as porcupine grass. The fynbos, which has few trees, is comprised mostly of large shrubs, especially heathers and a group of closely related plants known as proteas. Protea plants bear exquisite flowers.

Flowery Wonderland

Like the desert, the chaparral is dull-colored for much of the year. When conditions are right, however, it comes alive with myriad colorful flowers. The maquis is dotted with the yellow blooms of gorse and the white blossoms of shadbush. In the mallee scrub, eucalyptus trees carry flowers that are massive puffs of red. Between the end of January and the beginning of May, the California chaparral gleams with the snow-white blooms of the whipple yucca. The blooms top stalks that grow up to 15 feet (5 meters) high. In June, the California fremontia paints the chaparral landscape with large flowers of brilliant yellow.

Proteas symbolize the flowery wonderland of the fynbos. These plants are named after Proteus, an ancient god who was worshiped by some Mediterranean peoples. Proteus was

There are many different kinds of protea flowers, such as these large, pink blooms seen in South Africa.

believed to have the ability to assume an endless number of disguises and even to change shape. Proteas come in many different shapes and sizes, from small trees to tiny plants that spread like mats over the ground. Many bear huge flowers of gorgeous colors, while others produce flowers that are miniscule. Some protea flowers resemble roses. Others are shaped like thistles, pencils, softballs, and pincushions. Their colors include pink, apricot, silver, yellow, red, and green.

The spectacular whipple yucca has large blooms that tower above the chaparral.

The South African fynbos is truly a wonderland of flowers. It is home to more than 8,000 species of flowering plants—about 6,000 of which exist nowhere else on Earth. Outside Capetown, South Africa, the slopes and flat top of towering Table Mountain are a botanical treasure house of 1,400 species of flowers.

Some of the most gorgeous flowers in the fynbos besides the proteas are the orchids. Some species inhabit only a few areas. The small blue drip disa orchid lives in the damp crevices and among the moss of Table Mountain—and only there. Another species native to Table Mountain and a few other mountainous areas is the red disa, which is commonly called the flower of the gods. It grows more than 1.5 feet (0.5 meter) and carries five or more blossoms, each about 10 inches (25 centimeters) wide.

EACH TO ITS OWN

Altitude and soil, as well as other factors, can determine where different types of chaparral grow within one geographical area. In California, montane chaparral grows in soils that are shallow to deep on slopes that range from gentle to steep and face any direction. Because chaparral favors slightly cooler temperatures, in northern California it is found at elevations of 3,000 to 9,000 feet (915 to 2,745 meters), while in southern California the chaparral does not grow below 7,000 feet (2,135 meters).

Mixed chaparral occurs in many different settings, but at lower elevations it grows mostly on slopes that face north and, thus, are cooler. It usually grows on steep ridges and slopes with thin soils that are often rocky, gravelly, or sandy. It is seldom seen on slopes above 5,500 feet (1,678 meters).

Chamiso-redshank chaparral usually grows at lower elevations than mixed chaparral. However, it also favors steep ridges and slopes. The chamiso can tolerate very thin, poor soils and heat, which is one reason it is often found on slopes that face to the south and the southwest.

Survival Experts

Like desert plants, those of the chaparral must be able to cope with long periods of heat and drought. Both have many of the same adaptations to survive these conditions. The growth of chaparral plants is closely related to how much moisture is available in the ground. Many annuals with shallow roots, which live for a season and then go to seed, sprout from seeds and start growing furiously as soon as the first rains come. Their shallow roots are able to absorb water near the surface, which is where moisture is concentrated early in the rainy season. Growth is at a maximum, and the plants flower during early spring, when the soil holds the greatest amount of moisture. The seeds mature after the rains, when the hot, dry summer begins. The seeds remain dormant for the summer and then come to life when the rains begin. Plants such as these, which need little or no water when it is scarce, are called drought avoiders. Other types of drought avoiders are those plants that drop their leaves during the summer. Leaves take in and release large amounts of moisture. If a plant has no leaves, it needs a minimal amount of moisture.

LEAVES OF THREE

Poison ivy and its relative poison oak—which is actually not an oak—are quite common in the chaparral. Their sap contains an oily chemical called urushiol. At least seven out of ten people are allergic to urushiol and develop an itchy rash when they come into contact with it.

It takes two exposures to urushiol to produce a rash. On the first exposure, the body learns to recognize the chemical but does not develop a rash. On the second exposure, an itchy rash appears if the person is allergic to the chemical. Yet even people who are not allergic to urushiol one year may develop the allergy the following year. However, the more time that elapses from one contact to the next with urushiol, the less sensitive that person will be to it. Frequent exposure has the opposite effect—it will make each reaction worse.

Merely brushing against poison ivy or poison oak can cause exposure to urushiol. The sap oozes through even the slightest break in stems, vines, berries, or leaves. Urushiol molecules quickly penetrate the skin, especially the soft parts, such as between the fingers.

Urushiol can also be picked up secondhand; for example, from clothing and pets that have been in contact with poison ivy. It can also be carried in smoke. Exposure to urushiol in smoke from burning poison ivy and poison oak is dangerous, especially if the smoke enters the eyes or the lungs. This kind of exposure is a major problem for firefighters in burning chaparral.

Most leaves of the poison ivy or poison oak plant are divided into three leaflets. Poison ivy leaflets are usually shaped like arrowheads. Those of poison oak resemble oak leaves, but the leaves vary in shape and number of leaflets. Therefore, it can be difficult to identify poison oak. A poison oak leaf, for example, may have as many as eleven leaflets. All of the leaves, however, will have an oily appearance. They are deep green in

In contrast, most evergreen shrubs, which have deep roots, do not start their growth cycle until well after the rainy season, when water has penetrated deep into the ground. These plants generally bear small leaves. Their small surface reduces water loss. What surface they do have is leathery and tough, which further reduces water loss. Evergreen shrubs do not drop their leaves, although some have fewer leaves in summer than during the moist winter. These plants are known as summer and red or yellow in fall. Poison ivy and poison oak are easiest to identify in fall and winter, when they bear clusters of waxy white berries.

Poison ivy grows throughout most of the country, especially in the East and the Midwest. Poison oak is less abundant, except along the Pacific Coast, where it can be one of the most numerous small plants around. Both grow as vines, creepers, or even low shrubs.

Poison ivy and poison oak like sunlight. They find it along the sides of roads, trails, and streams. Unused clearings, or hay fields and pastures that have started to overgrow, are other good spots for them to thrive. In the woods, they reach for sunlight by climbing tree trunks.

Like all other living things, poison ivy and poison oak have their place in nature. Quail, chicadees, flickers, mockingbirds, warblers, pocket mice, and wood rats eat the berries. Mule deer feed on the foliage and twigs. Bees take nectar from the flowers to make honey.

Poison ivy leaflets are usually shaped like arrowheads and have white clusters of fruit.

Poison oak leaflets are often shaped like oak leaves and also have white clusters of fruit.

drought tolerators. Chamiso is one of these plants. It is also known as greasewood for one of the ways in which it protects itself against water loss. The small, narrow leaves of chamiso excrete a waxy substance that covers them and holds moisture. This grease is highly flammable and burns much like oil, producing an intensely hot flame and thick clouds of black smoke. The chamiso plant is one of the reasons that wildfires burn so intensely in the chaparral.

3

Fire and the Chaparral

When explorer Vasco da Gama visited the southern cape of Africa, now known as the Cape of Good Hope, he called it Terra de Fume or "Cape of Fire." The land was ablaze with the smoke and flames of burning fynbos vegetation. Fire is not unusual in the chaparral, which is highly flammable. Those who governed the Europeans who had settled the fynbos region of South Africa took note of this fact when the settlers began to burn the vegetation in order to improve grazing for their cattle. People who burned the land in an unregulated fashion were subject to severe penalties—even execution. Fire, however, is not necessarily bad for the chaparral. In fact, many scientists believe that fire causes changes that are key environmental influences on chaparral vegetation.

**Opposite:
Fire is key to
the health and
survival of the
chaparral.**

The Changing Face of Nature

Natural communities—the plants and animals that make up an environment—experience gradual change. Change occurs owing to a variety of factors, including weather and the growth of plants. New plants may move into an area. A disease may wipe out certain species of animals or plants. A great storm may level forests, as Hurricane Hugo did in the southeastern United States in 1989. Fire may kill plants and animals.

As these transformations and others take place, the plants and animals of a community also change, sometimes so radically that new communities are formed. This process is known as succession.

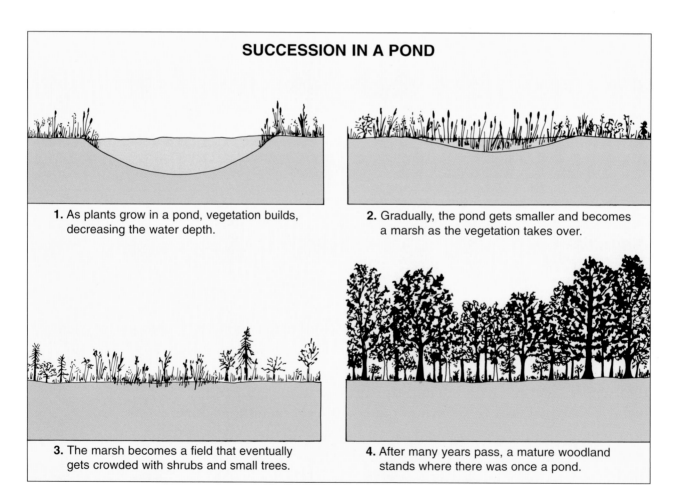

SUCCESSION IN A POND

1. As plants grow in a pond, vegetation builds, decreasing the water depth.

2. Gradually, the pond gets smaller and becomes a marsh as the vegetation takes over.

3. The marsh becomes a field that eventually gets crowded with shrubs and small trees.

4. After many years pass, a mature woodland stands where there was once a pond.

Succession may take many years, sometimes even centuries. A vivid example of succession is the development of a woodland from a small lake. In its original state, the lake is the home of fish, such as sunfish and largemouth bass, as well as frogs and turtles. Ducks paddle over its surface. Aquatic plants grow on the floor of the lake, most thickly near the shoreline. As the years pass, dead vegetation begins to build up on the bottom, decreasing the depth of the water. Leaves that fall from nearby trees also pile up in the lake. As the lake becomes more shallow, the number and variety of plants that can grow in it increases. Cattails and sedges take root on the lake's edges, gradually marching into the shallows. Eventually, the lake becomes a marshy pond, thick with vegetation and too shallow for fish. Cattails, frogs, and turtles take over.

More years pass. As plants grow and die, the watery area of the marsh shrinks and the frogs and turtles disappear. Eventually, what was a lake becomes a meadow with scattered shrubs. Rabbits, mice, and songbirds arrive. Little by little, the seeds of maples and oaks sprout on the meadow and grow into trees. In the end, a woodland stands on the spot. As more years pass, the woodland becomes a mature stand of forest. If left undisturbed, the mature forest will not be replaced by another community. This is the final, or climax, stage of the succession process.

Chaparral vegetation is not particularly long-lived, but it grows quickly and reaches its climax stage in about ten years. Some scientists believe that, in the long run, the vegetation of undisturbed climax chaparral becomes so thick that it begins to choke itself—new plants do not have a chance to grow underneath the tangled greenery above. Much of the chaparral vegetation is short-lived compared with other plants, such as large trees. Without the growth of young chaparral-type plants, and with the death of mature individuals, the chaparral species could disappear. According to this scenario, other plant communities, such as oak woods and coniferous forests,

The greasewood plant burns quickly, thus shielding nearby seeds from the traveling fire.

could replace the chaparral. Without periodic wildfires to clear away the old vegetation and allow young chaparral plants eventually to return, chaparral communities would disappear.

Not all scientists who have studied the chaparral agree. However, not one disputes the fact that periodic fires—as long as they do not occur too frequently—renew and preserve the life of the chaparral. Ironically, in the chaparral, fire can fight fire. Dead, dry chaparral vegetation, such as greasewood, burns quickly and intensely, often at a temperature of more than 1,000°F (537°C), and is consumed in a flash. Because the fire travels so quickly, its heat does not penetrate into the soil, so seeds and small animals that have taken shelter there are not harmed. If too much dead vegetation accumulates, though, fires burn longer, killing organisms under the ground as well as above it.

Natural wildfires, which are started by lightning, periodically burn through the chaparral. In California, the frequency of these fires seems to be every ten to forty years. However, people have upset that time frame. In many parts of California, fires set by accident—or by arsonists—occur so often that the ecological balance of the chaparral is disturbed. Nonetheless, in other areas, land-management authorities sometimes set controlled fires in chaparral that they believe has gone too long without burning. Scientists are still trying to figure out how to balance human activities with the natural occurrence of fire in the chaparral.

A ranger starts a prescribed burn that controls the limits of the fire.

DOUBLING THEIR CHANCES

Some chaparral plants, such as the mallee trees of Australia, the proteas of South Africa, and several types of pine found in and near the California chaparral, retain their seeds for a long period of time in such structures as the cones of the pine. Torrey pines, coulter pines, and digger pines are closely associated with chaparral in many areas because they can tolerate a dry climate and poor soil. They are the only plants in the chaparral that store their seeds aboveground as well as in the soil. The scales of their cones are tightly sealed by pine resin. Some of the cones open when mature, like those of most other pines, and the seeds fall to the ground, where some survive and sprout. But these pines always retain some cones that stay closed, protecting the seeds, for several years. When a fire occurs, the heat melts the resin. A short time after the fire, the cones open, releasing a new crop of seeds to start another generation of pines.

Rising from the Ashes

Many plant species of the chaparral have evolved many adaptations that help them regrow after a fire. Many have seeds or bulbs that lie dormant in the soil for long periods of time, even for a hundred years or more. These seeds sprout, and the seedlings grow after fire clears away the cover of mature chaparral. Such plants as the California lilac and the manzanita establish large reservoirs of seeds in the soil and are able to rapidly return after a fire. The seeds of some chaparral flora, such as the fire lily of South Africa, cannot even sprout unless the heat of a fire splits their tough outer coverings, allowing moisture to enter. Other seeds do not sprout without undergoing chemical changes caused by heat from burning wood.

Still other plants, such as chamiso, have structures called burls at their bases that bud after a fire. The burls begin to grow when the plant is still a seedling. Scientists believe that chemicals in the plant prevent the burls from budding until a fire kills the stems of the plant.

A red-barked manzanita shrub can regenerate after a fire.

California lilac plants have large reservoirs of stored seeds that allow them to regrow after a fire.

Fire Followers

Within months of a chaparral fire, the bare earth shows evidence of the growth of a new generation of what scientists call fire-following plants. It is in the spring following a fire that the chaparral is most colorful. Small flowering plants with soft stems, which may have a difficult time growing under mature chaparral, cover the ground like a multicolored carpet. In California, such flowers as snapdragons and whispering bells blaze into life. In South Africa, anemones, gladiolus, and lilies are at their showiest.

The blaze of the red fire lily appears only after a fire splits the outer covering of its seed, allowing moisture to enter.

After a few years, the numbers of these flowers begin to decrease as tough grasses invade the area. Next come small shrubs, which eventually create shade, further inhibiting the growth of soft-stemmed plants. Then the main plants of the chaparral, such as chamiso, begin to take over until, in about one decade, the chaparral looks much like it did before it was engulfed in a wall of flame.

In the spring following a fire, bronze pixie snapdragons bloom brightly.

35

4

Wildlife of the Chaparral

Elephants, kangaroos, wild boars, deer, and cougars: What do they have in common? All have been able to survive in the chaparral, although some have vanished from certain areas due to human activities that have disrupted their environment. There are a few elephants left in game parks in the fynbos; kangaroos roam the mallee scrub; small deer called guemals inhabit the chaparral of Chile; wild boars root about in the maquis; and cougars roam the chaparral of California.

Because the chaparral is a forest of sorts, has a desert-like climate, and contains patches of grassland, many of the animals that inhabit this biome also inhabit others. A few species, however, are found only or mostly in the chaparral.

Opposite:
A gray kangaroo, with a joey in her pouch, travels through the mallee scrub.

37

Suited to the Chaparral

In the fynbos, there lives a bird known as the protea seed-eater. As its name implies, it feeds only on protea seeds. The California thrasher, a relative of the mockingbird and the brown thrasher, lives almost entirely within that state's chaparral. This biome is a good home for the California thrasher, as the bird likes to feed on the ground, where the thick brush protects it. It also nests in low shrubs, like those of the chaparral. It has short wings, which are well suited to carrying it through thick vegetation. When it is frightened, however, it usually scurries away on the ground. The California quail, another ground bird, and the wrentit, which nests in thick, low scrub, are most abundant in the chaparral.

One of the few mammals that live solely in the chaparral is the grysbok, a small antelope that inhabits the fynbos. The grysbok measures only 22 inches (56 centimeters) high at the shoulder and weighs 25 pounds (11 kilograms). Its small body enables it to creep through thickets that would entrap larger animals. Grysbok usually move about slowly and hold their heads low. When it is frightened, a grysbok does not run, as do most other antelopes. Instead, it flattens itself on the ground with its neck outstretched, which is a perfect strategy for hiding in thick vegetation. The shy grysbok will even hide in the deep burrows of aardvarks.

A tiny grysbok is captured on film in South Africa.

A Mixture of Mammals

Unlike the grysbok, most of the animals that inhabit the chaparral also inhabit other biomes. Occasionally, however, the individuals that dwell in the chaparral differ slightly in behavior or appearance from members of their species that live elsewhere. For example, the two largest kangaroos in Australia are the red kangaroo and the great gray kangaroo. The great gray kangaroo is 7 feet (2 meters) high and 9 feet (3 meters) long. The red kangaroo, however, is slightly smaller. It is a creature of the open plains, where there is little rainfall. The great gray kangaroo, which is also called a forester, prefers forest with regular rainfall or a winter rainy season, as in the mallee scrub. The red kangaroo is the more graceful leaper of the two, as suits an animal of the open country. The great gray kangaroo is usually bulkier. Great gray kangaroos from different parts of Australia exhibit some differences in coloration. The mallee kangaroo is also known as the black-faced kangaroo because of the dark color of its muzzle.

The mallee scrub is one of the areas of Australia in which wild dogs called dingoes are very common. These large dogs are also found on open grasslands and, to some extent, in deep

In South Africa, a family of chacma baboons plays in the fynbos.

forests. Scientists believe that dingoes are domesticated dogs brought to Australia in prehistoric times by the ancestors of the Australian Aborigines and that they eventually ran wild.

Most of the fynbos region of South Africa has been heavily developed by people for hundreds of years. Because of this, many of the larger animals that inhabited the area, such as lions, are gone. However, many of them may still be found in the back country and in nature preserves. These include leopards, chacma baboons, mountain zebra, and such antelope as bontebock. Elephants once roamed much of the fynbos. A small herd can still be seen at the edge of fynbos country in the Addo Elephant National Park.

In Spain's Parque Nacional de Doñana, macchia is a favored territory of the Spanish lynx, an endangered wild cat. Only about 1,000 of these cats remain, all in the delta of the Guadalquivir River and a few mountainous areas. The numbers of lynx dropped sharply during the 1950s, when the rabbits on which they fed were decimated by disease. Since then, these cats have relied on other small mammals for food, such as hares and ground birds, including partridges. Parque Nacional de Doñana is also home to another rare feline, the European wildcat. Many other mammals also live in the area, including red deer, fallow deer, and wild boars.

The rugged macchia-covered mountains of the Mediterranean islands of Corsica and Sardinia are the last natural homes of the mouflon, a European wild sheep. Thousands of years ago, it lived throughout much of Europe, but in modern times its range has dwindled to these two islands. During the past two centuries, however, the mouflon has been reintroduced in several game parks on the European mainland.

As seen here in Austria, mouflon have been reintroduced to the European mainland.

THE TEMPERATURE TAKER

In Australia, there lives a large ground bird with an interesting nesting habit. It is almost always found in or near mallee scrub. Called the mallee fowl, it belongs to a family of birds called mound builders because they put their eggs under mounds of vegetation. The eggs are incubated not only by the heat of the sun, but also by the heat of the vegetation as it decays.

Around May, which is autumn in Australia, the male mallee fowl digs a large pit in the ground. It is between 2 to 3 feet (0.6 to 0.9 meter) deep and up to 16 feet (5 meters) in diameter. From then until July, the male scrapes dry twigs and leaves into the pit. By August, the winter rainy season has soaked the vegetation, and it is decaying. The male forms a mound up to 12 inches (30 centimeters) above ground level. Then he digs a hole in the center of the mound and caps it with sand and leaves.

When the female is ready to lay an egg, the male digs out the hole. It may take him two hours to do so, since he may have to excavate up to a cubic yard of soil. After the egg is in the hole, the male then covers the hole once again.

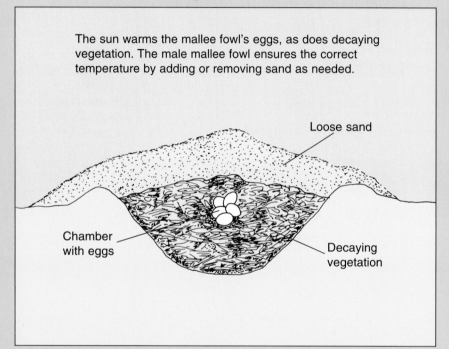

The sun warms the mallee fowl's eggs, as does decaying vegetation. The male mallee fowl ensures the correct temperature by adding or removing sand as needed.

Loose sand

Chamber with eggs

Decaying vegetation

Mouflons eat a wide variety of plants and can easily survive on the tough vegetation of the macchia. So can the ibex, or wild goat, which holds out in a few mountainous areas of Spain and a few islands in the eastern Mediterranean, such as Crete. It also lives in mountainous areas outside the chaparral biome, such as the Alps.

The California chaparral teems with mammals, ranging from such large species as mule deer to such small ones as grasshopper mice and kangaroo rats. During the summer,

Several females may lay their eggs in the nest, and the total number of eggs can reach thirty-five. The male does a huge amount of digging and filling during a single nesting season. Egg laying usually starts in September. Each egg needs seven weeks to incubate, so those produced first hatch before the last are put in the egg chamber. The last young fowls usually hatch and dig themselves out of the mound in March and April.

By filling his bill with sand, a male mallee fowl measures the temperature in the egg chamber.

The correct temperature for incubation is 92°F (33°C). Since the eggs incubate under the hot spring and summer sun, the temperature in the mound can easily climb to higher than that. The male mallee fowl, however, is able to regulate the temperature of the egg chamber. He removes hot sand and replaces it with cool sand. In case of cold weather, he adds more soil and vegetation to the mound in order to raise the temperature inside.

How does the mallee fowl gauge the temperature in the mound? Male mallee fowl often fill their bills with sand from inside the mound. Scientists believe that sense organs in the bird's bill or tongue enable it to determine the temperature of the sand.

mule deer generally migrate to the higher slopes, above 6,000 feet (1,830 meters), to escape the heat.

Deer are the main prey of a predator that has become increasingly common in the chaparral. The cougar, or mountain lion, is a very reclusive creature, and the dense thickets of chaparral provide it with the hiding places it requires. Under cover of the chaparral, cougars sometimes roam the fringes of large cities, such as Los Angeles. Another reclusive cat, the bobcat, also inhabits the chaparral. However, the predator that

The chaparral provides the cougar, a very powerful predator, with dense hiding places.

is most abundant in the chaparral, as it is in many other areas, is the coyote. Coyotes prey on such creatures as brush rabbits and ground squirrels.

Wings Over the Chaparral

As is true of mammals, the birds that inhabit the chaparral include many species that also make their home in other biomes. The many small mammals of the chaparral biome attract large numbers of hawks and eagles. Soaring over the California chaparral are golden eagles, sharp-shinned hawks, and red-tailed hawks. In Europe, the macchia also draws many hawks and eagles. The golden eagle, Bonelli's eagle and the imperial eagle hunt in the macchia of Parque Nacional de Doñana. Many hawks and eagles leave the chaparral during the hottest times of the year.

A red-tailed hawk displays the feathers that give this bird of prey its name.

A roadrunner clutches an American collared lizard in its beak.

A black-billed cuckoo feeds its young.

Other birds common in the European chaparral are the stonechat, nightjar, jackdaw, green woodpecker, and cuckoo. In parts of Greece, the macchia is enlivened by the music of some especially melodious songbirds, such as the stone nuthatch and the blackcap. Roadrunners, ground birds that feed largely on snakes and lizards and that are prevalent in deserts, also live in the chaparral of California. In fact, they are so abundant that the early pioneers called them chaparral cocks. In California, the presence of oak trees in the chaparral attracts large numbers of scrub jays. These birds consume large quantities of acorns. Like squirrels, they bury the acorns, many of which sprout and produce new oaks.

Snakes Alive!

As they are in deserts, reptiles are numerous in the chaparral. In Europe, these include the leopard snake, the arrow snake, and the Montpellier snake. The Montpellier snake has very powerful venom but is not considered particularly

47

dangerous to humans. Its fangs are far back in its jaws and thus are not in a position to deliver a bite to a large animal. It feeds on small creatures, such as lizards and nesting birds, which it engulfs in its jaws and pierces with its fangs.

The venomous snakes with the most effective fangs belong to the Viperidae family. Their long fangs, located in the front of the upper jaw, contain channels through which venom flows when the snake strikes. When not in use, the fangs rest in a lowered position in the jaw. When the snake strikes, a bone in its jaw rotates and the fangs are raised so that they point forward. The snake stabs its victim with its fangs.

Rattlesnakes are among the most abundant snakes found in the California chaparral. Their species include the western rattlesnake, the red diamond rattlesnake, and the speckled rattlesnake. They feed mostly on small mammals, such as ground

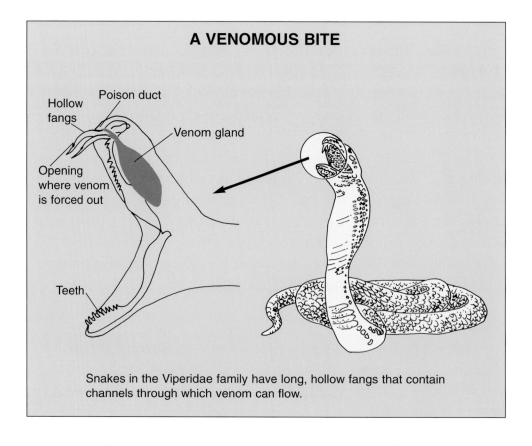

A VENOMOUS BITE

Hollow fangs

Poison duct

Venom gland

Opening where venom is forced out

Teeth

Snakes in the Viperidae family have long, hollow fangs that contain channels through which venom can flow.

squirrels and rats. Rattlesnakes hunt by night with the aid of two unusual organs. Pits on each side of a rattlesnake's snout contain structures that can sense the body heat given off by mammals. Another organ on the roof of the rattlesnake's mouth can detect the odor of chemical particles left behind by a passing animal. The rattler picks up these particles with its tongue and transports them to the sense organ. In this way, it is able to trail its prey.

Rattlesnakes can be dangerous to people, but they attack humans only when they are alarmed or surprised. Because they consume vast numbers of rodents, they actually do humans an important service.

Rattlesnakes, such as this red diamond, have pits on each side of their snouts that sense the body heat of mammals.

5

The Chaparral and People

In much of the world, the chaparral has been greatly affected by human activities. This is especially true in the Mediterranean, in South Africa, and in California. Some activities have benefited the chaparral, while others have had a very harmful effect.

Macchia Rules

One of the regions in which human activities have encouraged the spread of the chaparral biome is along the Mediterranean rim of Europe. However, the European chaparral, or macchia, has extended its boundaries at the expense of other plant communities that have been destroyed by people.

Opposite:
The Cape
Peninsula in
South Africa is
a populated area
of chaparral.

Macchia has probably always existed close to the coast of Mediterranean lands. Thousands of years ago, however, open, sun-splashed forests of large oaks and other deciduous trees, as well as pines, cedars, and cypresses, grew over most of the inland areas, extending up steep mountain slopes thousands of feet high. Today, almost all of those forests are gone. In many places where they once grew, macchia rules the land.

The destruction of Mediterranean forests began long ago, perhaps more than 3,000 years ago. As the cradle of civilization, the Mediterranean was more densely populated than other parts of Europe were. Forests were cut down for timber and leveled by axes and fire to create grazing land. Cattle and goats destroyed most of the vegetation that remained.

Much of the land in this area was mountainous and rocky. Once the forests were destroyed, wind and water eroded the soil. Erosion was particularly bad on steep slopes. The soil became thin and poor. Without trees and their leaf litter, it could not again become fertile. Macchia, however, is able to grow in thin, desertlike soil, so it climbed the slopes and invaded the ravaged forest land. The ancient forests had been in a climax stage of succession. By destroying the forests, people triggered an entirely new process of succession whose climax stage was macchia.

Land at Africa's Tip

South Africa was settled by Europeans, chiefly of Dutch descent, in the seventeenth century. Initial settlement was in the Cape region, where fynbos is found. Gradually, large areas of fynbos were turned into agricultural and grazing lands. Later, cities, towns, and industries developed.

The fynbos region once had a great population of wild animals, including such large species as elephants, buffalo, lions, zebras, and a relative of the zebra called the quagga. The quagga and the Cape lion became extinct as the number of humans in the area increased. Elephants were pushed out of

The quagga had stripes only on its head, neck, and forebody. It has been extinct since 1883.

the area because they destroyed the farms. Animal life in South Africa's fynbos region in general declined.

Even so, there are many areas of the fynbos in which wild animals continue to thrive. Leopards, which tolerate the presence of people better than lions do, still prowl mountainous areas. The fynbos teems with birds. Moreover, South Africa has established one of the world's best systems of national parks as well as game preserves, both public and private. South African president Nelson Mandela has pledged not only to keep this system operating but to make it better.

Addo Elephant Park, near the fynbos belt, contains a healthy elephant population, as well as endangered black rhinoceroses and buffalo. It is a reminder of what the Cape

The endangered black rhinoceros is protected in Addo Elephant Park in South Africa.

looked like when the Europeans first landed. A mecca for bird-watchers is Tsitsikamma Coastal National Park, where fynbos grows on ridges and plateaus above the sea. The Cape of Good Hope Nature Reserve contains more than 1,000 species of fynbos plants as well as the rare mountain zebra and eight types of antelope. These are just a few of the preserves in the region, and more will undoubtedly be developed in the future. In South Africa, people have destroyed areas of fynbos, but they are working at preserving it.

The Cape of Good Hope Nature Reserve is home to the rare mountain zebra.

Striking a Balance

Ecologists and others concerned with the California chaparral face a constant battle. They must continually strike a balance between too much fire and not enough. Because of human activities, fires burn more frequently in the chaparral

55

than they did when the only inhabitants of the region were Native Americans. The problem is most severe where housing developments—and there are many—have been placed deep in the chaparral or have surrounded it. The more development occurs in the chaparral, the more likely it is that accidental fires will occur. Some wildfires have burned hundreds of thousands of acres. On a regular basis, uncontrolled chaparral fires in California threaten or destroy homes and other buildings and sometimes take human life. Hundreds of homes have been lost in a single wildfire. Photographs in newspapers, magazines, and television reports show sheets of flame, whipped by winds, eating through a tangle of tinder-dry vegetation. Firefighters battle the blazing brush at the risk of their own lives. Residents must flee from their homes, often leaving all their belongings to be consumed by the raging fire. Some of these fires begin naturally, some occur because of human carelessness, and still others are set by arsonists.

The increased population of the California chaparral has led to more frequent fires, upsetting the balance of the biome.

People have been in contact with the chaparral since the first Native Americans reached the California region in prehistoric times. Historians and scientists are uncertain about how much the native peoples of California burned chaparral to provide clearings and drive game animals. It is generally believed, however, that burning by Native Americans was limited.

After the Spaniards and, later, other Americans arrived, large areas of chaparral were destroyed. Grazing animals ravaged it, and ranchers continually burned the vegetation so that grass would grow. Fires were set so frequently that some parts of the chaparral could not regenerate. As time passed, settlers poured into regions of the chaparral that had previously been uninhabited by humans.

In 1991, more than 3,300 homes were destroyed and 1,600 acres (648 hectares) burned in a fire in the developed chaparral of California.

WINGS OF THE CONDOR

The condor is the largest bird of prey in North America.

The largest bird of prey in North America—and the largest flying bird on the planet—is a native of the rocky, mountainous back country of the California chaparral. It is the California condor, an immense vulture with a wingspan of more than 10 feet (3 meters). The condor, which feeds on carrion, is a relic of prehistoric times. It was prevalent when saber-toothed cats and mastodons lived in California. They are gone, but the condor continues to survive—barely.

Never abundant in modern times, the condor was on the verge of extinction by the 1980s. Large areas of its habitat had been disrupted by people, which interfered with the giant birds' nesting. Many condors died from eating such prey as coyotes that had been poisoned to control the population. Some were shot illegally.

With little time to spare, conservative biologists joined forces to save this species. They began to remove condor eggs and the birds themselves from the wild. The last wild condor was captured in 1987. The birds were bred in zoos, and their numbers increased. During the early 1990s, scientists began to release the condors, a few at a time, into the wild. Now a handful of condors once again fly over the chaparral.

It remains to be seen whether these birds, which were bred in captivity, will survive in the wild.

Today, millions of people live in and near the California chaparral. For many years, land managers, forestry officials, and public-safety authorities concentrated on preventing and putting out chaparral fires. This was a two-edged sword, however, because the suppression of fires caused a buildup of dead vegetation, which in turn increased the likelihood of subsequent fires, which, once started, were more severe. Even so, for most of this century, state and federal government agencies in California concentrated on stopping fire in the chaparral, rather than using it as a fire-fighting tool.

Gradually, this attitude changed. Scientists began conducting experiments in selected areas of the chaparral. They created controlled test burns to determine how the fires could be managed and what would happen afterward. Today, the California Department of Forestry and Fire Protection and such federal agencies as the U.S. Bureau of Land Management and the U.S. Forest Service regularly conduct prescribed burning in the chaparral.

The Department of Forestry and Fire Protection works closely with private landowners to reduce the fire hazard caused by the buildup of dead vegetation, especially when it is near buildings. The department is also involved with burning on state property and works closely with federal agencies, such as the U.S. Bureau of Land Management, which is responsible for large tracts of land where chaparral grows.

Prescribed burning is planned and carried out with extreme care. Environmental regulations covering the impact of smoke in the air and damage to wildlife must be considered. Weather conditions are taken into account. Fire-fighting equipment and personnel are on hand at the burn site to prevent the fire from going out of control.

Prescribed burning may sound like tinkering with nature, but there are few places on Earth where nature has not been touched by people and their actions. Therefore, humans must work with nature to keep the natural world in balance.

Glossary

adaptation A characteristic of an organism that makes it suited to live or reproduce in a particular environment.

biome A community of specific types of plants, animals, and other organisms that covers a large area of the earth.

burl A structure in the roots of some plants that contains buds.

climax The final stage of succession.

fynbos The chaparral of South Africa's Cape of Good Hope.

garigue A low form of chaparral in Europe.

halimium A common heath plant.

heath An area covered by coarse, shrubby plants.

macchia A thick variety of European chaparral.

mallee scrub An Australian type of chaparral dominated by dwarf eucalyptus trees.

maquis Another term for macchia.

matorral A word used in Chile for chaparral.

montane Refers to mountains, as in montane chaparral.

natural community The plants and animals in a habitat.

parasite An organism that lives off another organism.

predator An animal that hunts other animals to eat them.

prey An animal that is eaten by another animal.

Proteus An ancient Mediterranean god who had many disguises and could change shape; the protea flower is named for this god.

reproduction The process by which an organism creates new individuals of the same species.

succession A natural process that occurs over time by which one community of organisms is replaced by other communities until a stable, long-lasting community, called a climax community, is established.

urushiol A chemical in the sap of poison ivy and poison oak that causes an allergic reaction in many people.

For Further Reading

Behme, Robert L. *Incredible Plants: Oddities, Curiosities & Eccentricities*. New York: Sterling, 1992.

Dolce, Laura. *Australia*. New York: Chelsea, 1990.

Kaplan, Elizabeth. *Taiga*. New York: Marshall Cavendish, 1996.

_____. *Temperate Forest*. New York: Marshall Cavendish, 1996.

Landau, Elaine. *Cowboys*. New York: Franklin Watts, 1990.

Lepthien, Emilie U. *Australia*. New York: Childrens Press, 1982.

Paige, David. *A Day in the Life of a Forest Ranger*. Mahwah, NJ: Troll, 1980.

Ricciuti, Edward. *Birds*. Woodbridge, CT: Blackbirch Press, 1993.

_____. *Desert*. New York: Marshall Cavendish, 1996.

_____. *Grassland*. New York: Marshall Cavendish, 1996.

_____. *Reptiles*. Woodbridge, CT: Blackbirch Press, 1993.

Index

Acorns, 18
Addo Elephant Park, 40, 53, 54
Air pollution, 59
Altitude, effect on chaparral, 23
Animals. *See* Wildlife
Antelope, 40, 55

Baboons, 40
Biomes, 4–5
Birds. *See also* Wildlife
    common to chaparral, 38, 44–47
    condor, 58
    mallee fowl, 42–43
    places to see, 55
Bitter cherry, 20 (photo)
Blackcaps, 47
Bobcats, 43
Bontebock antelope, 40
Buffalo, 52, 53

California lilacs, 32, 33 (photo)
California quails, 38
California thrashers, 38
Chabarra, 15
Chacma baboons, 40 (photo)
Chamiso, 20, 23, 25, 32, 35
Chamiso-redshank chaparral, 18.
    See also Chaparral
Chaparral. *See also* specific subject
    as biome, 4, 7–9
    countries' names for, 15
    destruction of, 57
    location of, 10–12
    overview, 9
    types, 17–20

Chaps, 15 (photo)
Climate
    of chaparral, 12, 13
    importance to biomes, 5
Coastal scrub, 19–20
Condors, 58 (photo)
Cones, 32
Controlled fires, 31, 59
Cougars, 37, 43, 44 (photo)
Coyote brush, 20
Coyotes, 44
Cuckoos, 47 (photo)

Deer, mule, 42–43
Deforestation, 52
Deserts, 4, 12, 13
Dingoes, 39 (photo), 40
Dodder, 19

Eagles, 44
Ecologists, 4
Elephants, 13, 14 (photo), 37, 40,
    52–53
Erosion, 52
Eucalyptus trees, 20, 21
Evergreen shrubs, 24–25
Extinction, 52–55, 58

Fire, role in chaparral
    benefit of, 30
    effect on man, 56
    fighting fires, 50 (photo), 59
    frequency of, 55–56
    growth after, 33–35
    heat of, 25
    overview, 9, 27
    purposely set, 31, 59
    stunting effect on plants, 13
    succession, 28–29
Flowers, 16 (photo), 21–23. *See
    also* Plants
Forests, 4, 12. *See also* Plants
Fremontia, 21

Fynbos, 15, 20, 22, 27, 37, 38, 40, 52, 53, 55

Garigue, 19
Gorse, 21
Grasses, 9, 20
Grassland, as biome, 4
Greasewood, 25, 30 (photo)
Grysbok, 38 (photo)
Guemals, 37

Halimium, 10
Hawks, 44, 45 (photo)
Heathers, 20
Humans, role in chaparral. *See* People

Jackdaws, 47

Kalahari Desert, 12
Kangaroos, 13, 36 (photo), 37, 39

Leopards, 53
Lilies, 33, 34 (photo)
Lions, 52
Lynx, 40–41

Macchia, 10, 40, 41, 42, 44, 47, 51–52
Mallee fowl, 42–43 (photo)
Mallee scrub, 15, 20, 21, 32, 37, 39
Manzanita, 11 (photo), 18, 20, 32 (photo)
Maquis, 15, 37. *See also* Chaparral
Mediterranean climate, 9
Mistletoe, 19
Mixed chaparral, 20. *See also* Chaparral
Montane chaparral, 20, 23. *See also* Chaparral
Montpellier snake, 47–48
Mouflon sheep, 41 (photo), 42
Mountain lions, 43
Mountain mahogany, 20

Mule deer, 42–43

Native Americans, protection of chaparral, 57
Nightjars, 47

Oak trees, 15, 18, 20
Ocean, as biome, 4
Olive trees, 18
Orchids, 22

Parasites, plant, 19 (photo)
Parque Nacional de Doñana, 10, 40, 41, 44
People
    destruction of chaparral, 51–52
    fires and, 50 (photo), 56–57, 59
    protection of chaparral, 51, 59
Pine trees, 20, 32
Plants. *See also* specific plant or flower
    climate and, 5
    common to chaparral, 9–10, 17–20
    deforestation, 52
    dwarfing, 13
    fire, effect on. *See* Fire, role in chaparral
    flowers, 21–23
    heat and drought and, 23–25
    parasitic, 19
    succession and, 28–29
Poison ivy, 24–25
Poison oak, 20, 24–25
Pollution, air, 59
Porcupine grass, 20
Prescribed burning, 31 (photo), 59
Protea flowers, 20, 21 (photo), 22, 32
Protea seed-eater, 38

Quagga, 52–53 (photo)

Rain, 12, 13, 23
Rainforest, as biome, 4

Rattlesnakes, 48–49 (photo)
Rhinoceroses, 53, 54 (photo)
Roadrunners, 46 (photo), 47

Sagebrush, 20
Sahara Desert, 12
Scotch broom, 18 (photo)
Scrub oak, 8 (photo), 9
Shadbush, 18, 21
Snakes, 47–49
Snapdragons, 33, 35 (photo)
Soil, 13, 23
Stonechats, 47
Stone nuthatches, 47
Succession, 28–29
Sugar sumac, 18

Table Mountain, 22
Taiga, as biome, 4
Temperature. See Climate
Trees. See Plants
Tundra, as biome, 4

Urushiol, 24

Water, lack of, 23–25
Weather. See Climate
Whipple yucca, 21, 22 (photo)
Whitethorn ceanothus, 20
Wildcats, 41
Wildflowers, 16 (photo). See also
    Flowers
Wildlife. See also specific animal.
    See also Birds
        climate and, 5
        extinction and declining num-
            bers, 52–55, 58
        food for, 25
        mammals, 38–44
        overview, 13, 14, 37
        snakes, 47–49
        succession and, 28–29
Woodpeckers, 47

Yellow gorse, 18
Yucca, 20

Zebras, 40, 52, 55 (photo)

Acknowledgments and Photo Credits
Cover and pages 11, 33: ©Walter H. Hodge/Peter Arnold, Inc.; p. 6: ©Roland Birke/Peter Arnold, Inc.;
pp. 8, 34, 45: ©Stephen J. Krasemann/Peter Arnold, Inc.; p. 14: ©Mitch Reardon; p. 15: North Wind
Picture Archives; p. 16: ©Helga Lade/Peter Arnold, Inc.; pp. 18, 32: ©Verna R. Johnston/Photo
Researchers, Inc.; p. 19: ©Stephen P. Parker/Photo Researchers, Inc.; p. 20: ©Michael Luque/Photo
Researchers, Inc.; p. 21: ©Clyde H. Smith/Peter Arnold, Inc.; p. 22: ©Kathy Merrifield/Photo
Researchers, Inc.; pp. 26, 35: ©Richard Shiell/Earth Scenes; p. 30: ©Phil A. Dotson/Photo
Researchers, Inc.; p. 31: ©Roger Archibald/Earth Scenes; p. 36: ©John Cancalosi/Peter Arnold, Inc.;
p. 38: ©Anthony Bannister/Animals Animals; p. 39: ©Gerard Lacz/Peter Arnold, Inc.; p. 40: ©G. I.
Bernard/Oxford Scientific Films/Animals Animals; p. 41: ©Peter Weimann/Animals Animals; p. 43:
©Hans and Judy Beste/Animals Animals; pp. 44, 49, 58: ©Tom McHugh/Photo Researchers, Inc.; p.
46: ©Wyman Meinzer/Peter Arnold, Inc.; p. 47: ©Ralph A. Reinhold/Animals Animals; p. 50: ©H. R.
Bramaz/Peter Arnold, Inc.; p. 53: ©Animals Animals; p. 54: ©E. R. Degginger/Animals Animals; p. 55:
©Leonard Lee Rue III/Photo Researchers, Inc.; p. 56: ©Will and Deni McIntyre/Photo Researchers,
Inc.; p. 57: ©Dan Suzio/Photo Researchers, Inc.
Artwork by Blackbirch Graphics, Inc.

SPENCER LOOMIS SCHOOL
1 Hubbard Lane
Hawthorn Woods, IL 60047

DATE DUE

GAYLORD			PRINTED IN U.S.A.